Acknowledgements

The publishers would like to thank the following
for permission to reproduce photographs

Earth Images pp.4, 8, 16; Chris Fairclough pp.10, 28, 41;
FLPA pp.24, 28; Robert Harding p.40;
Hunting Aerofilms Ltd. p.26; Hutchison Library p.29;
Impact: Steve Benbow p.24, Robert Eames p.10,
Jean Hutchings p.10; Magnum Photos pp.42, 44;
Mark Mason Studios p.5; Mountain Camera:
Chris Bradley p.42, John Cleare pp.10, 28,
Colin Monteath p.29;
National Remote Sensing Centre (Airphotogroup) pp.2, 22;
Panos Pictures: Trygve Bolstad p.42;
Sealand Photography Ltd. p.26; Still Pictures pp.10, 44;
ZEFA p.10.

The globes on page 5 were supplied by
Cambridge Publishing Services.

The illustrations are by Chapman Bounford, Hardlines,
and Jon Riley.

Page design by Adrian Smith.

Cover image:
Tom Van Sant / Geosphere Project, Santa Monica ,
Science Photo Library.

OXFORD
UNIVERSITY PRESS

Great Clarendon Street, Oxford OX2 6DP

Oxford University Press is a department of the University of Oxford.
It furthers the University's objective of excellence in research, scholarship,
and education by publishing worldwide in

Oxford New York

Athens Auckland Bangkok Bogotá Buenos Aires Cape Town
Chennai Dar es Salaam Delhi Florence Hong Kong Istanbul Karachi
Kolkata Kuala Lumpur Madrid Melbourne Mexico City Mumbai Nairobi Paris
São Paulo Shanghai Singapore Taipei Tokyo Toronto Warsaw

with associated companies in Berlin Ibadan

Oxford is a registered trade mark of Oxford University Press
in the UK and in certain other countries

© Oxford University Press 1996

First published 1996
Reprinted 1996, 1997, with corrections 1998,
1999, 2000, 2001

© Maps copyright Oxford University Press

ISBN 0 19 831794 8 (paperback)   ISBN 0 19 831833 2 (hardback)

Printed in Italy by G. Canale & C. S.p.A.

THE
OXFORD
First
ATLAS

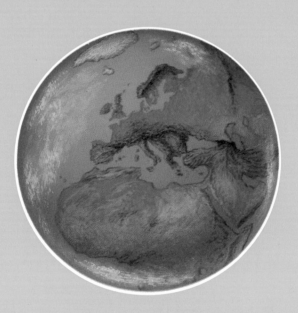

Editorial Adviser

Patrick Wiegand

Oxford University Press

2 Contents

Maps of the British Isles

Maps of the United Kingdom

Contents 3

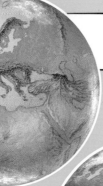
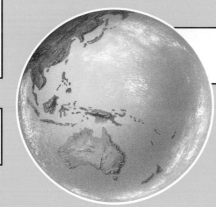
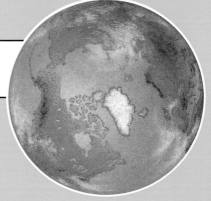
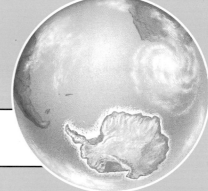
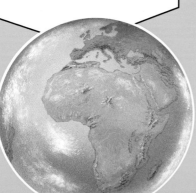
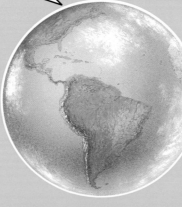

4 Planet Earth

The Earth is a **planet** in space.

It is round like a ball.

If you look at the Earth from space you can see land, sea, and clouds.

You cannot see countries.

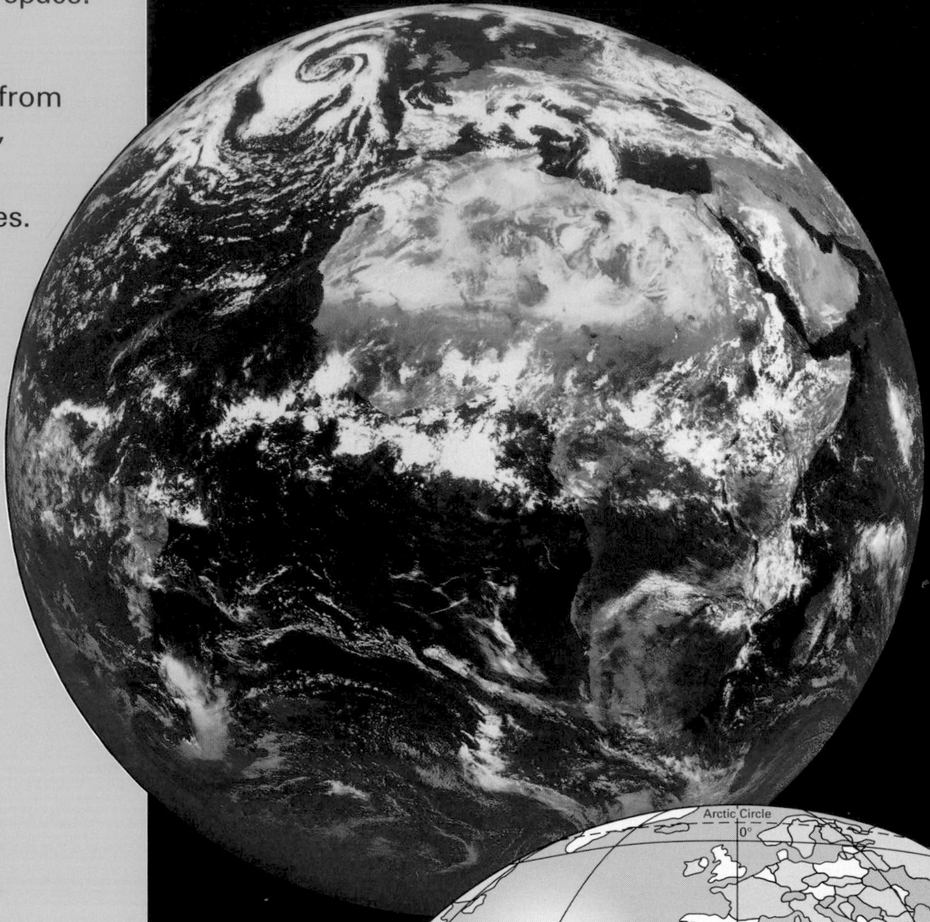

To see countries you need a map.

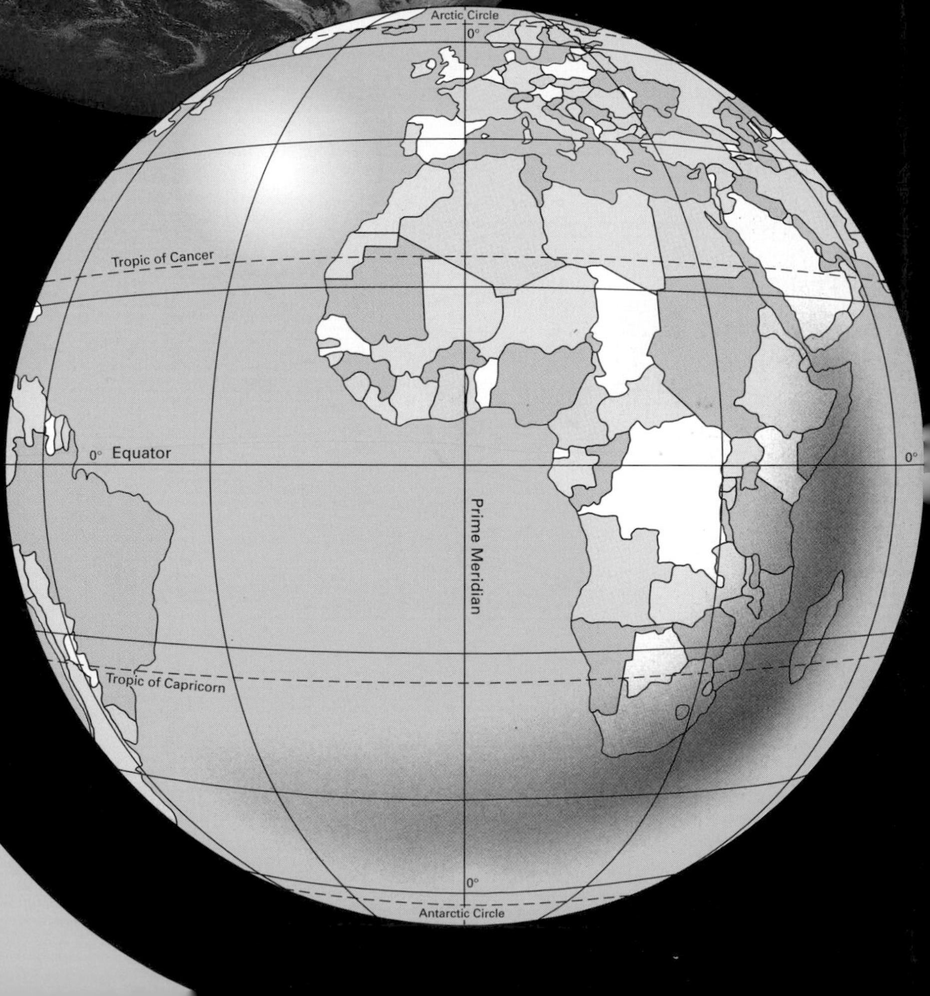

There are imaginary lines round the Earth. These help us describe where places are.

Some of the lines have special names.

The line around the middle of the Earth is called the **Equator**.

Arctic Circle

0°

Tropic of Cancer

0° Equator

0°

Prime Meridian

Tropic of Capricorn

0°

Antarctic Circle

A globe is a model of the Earth.

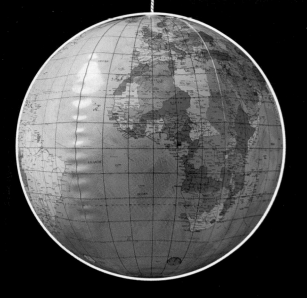

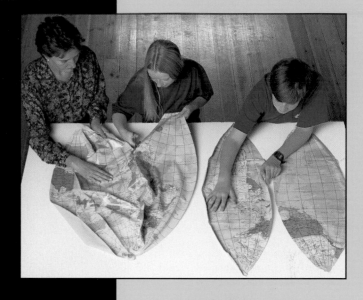

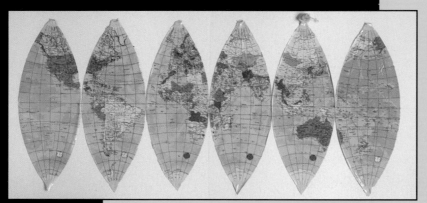

These strips have been cut from a globe and laid flat.

They make a world map.

The map is not easy to use because there are gaps in it.

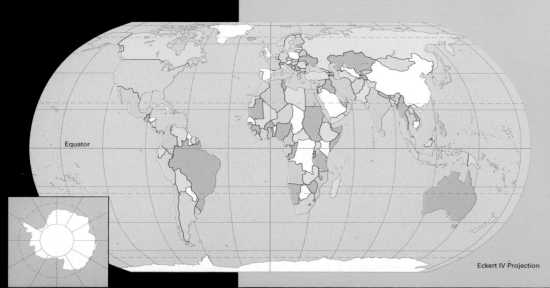

Equator

Here is a better world map. Some of the land shapes have had to be stretched.

A world map like this does not show Antarctica very well.

So Antarctica is shown here on a separate map.

Eckert IV Projection

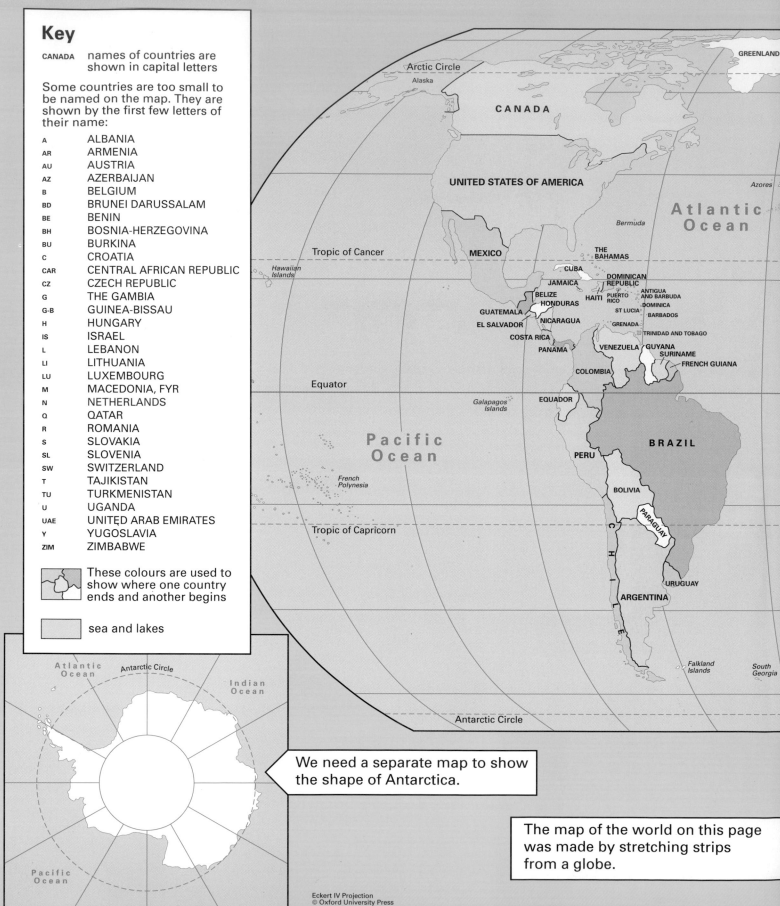

Key

CANADA   names of countries are shown in capital letters

Some countries are too small to be named on the map. They are shown by the first few letters of their name:

A	ALBANIA
AR	ARMENIA
AU	AUSTRIA
AZ	AZERBAIJAN
B	BELGIUM
BD	BRUNEI DARUSSALAM
BE	BENIN
BH	BOSNIA-HERZEGOVINA
BU	BURKINA
C	CROATIA
CAR	CENTRAL AFRICAN REPUBLIC
CZ	CZECH REPUBLIC
G	THE GAMBIA
G-B	GUINEA-BISSAU
H	HUNGARY
IS	ISRAEL
L	LEBANON
LI	LITHUANIA
LU	LUXEMBOURG
M	MACEDONIA, FYR
N	NETHERLANDS
Q	QATAR
R	ROMANIA
S	SLOVAKIA
SL	SLOVENIA
SW	SWITZERLAND
T	TAJIKISTAN
TU	TURKMENISTAN
U	UGANDA
UAE	UNITED ARAB EMIRATES
Y	YUGOSLAVIA
ZIM	ZIMBABWE

These colours are used to show where one country ends and another begins

sea and lakes

We need a separate map to show the shape of Antarctica.

The map of the world on this page was made by stretching strips from a globe.

Eckert IV Projection
© Oxford University Press

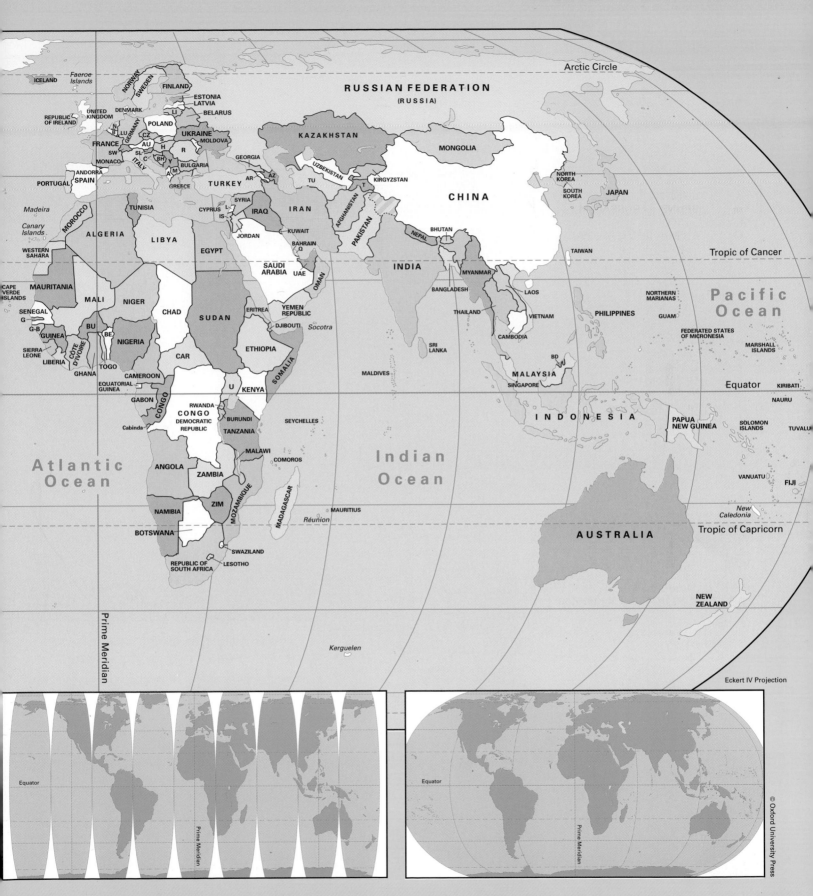

ICELAND
Faeroe Islands
Arctic Circle

NORWAY
SWEDEN
FINLAND
REPUBLIC OF IRELAND
UNITED KINGDOM
DENMARK
ESTONIA
LATVIA
LI
BELARUS

RUSSIAN FEDERATION (RUSSIA)

N
B
LUX
GERMANY
POLAND
UKRAINE
MOLDOVA
FRANCE
CZ
S
H
R
KAZAKHSTAN
MONGOLIA
AU
SL
BH
Y
BULGARIA
A
M
ITALY
MONACO
SW
C
ANDORRA
SPAIN
PORTUGAL
GREECE
TURKEY
GEORGIA
AR
AZ
UZBEKISTAN
TU
KIRGYZSTAN
NORTH KOREA
SOUTH KOREA
JAPAN

CHINA

MADEIRA
Madeira
Canary Islands
MOROCCO
TUNISIA
CYPRUS
IS
SYRIA
IRAQ
IRAN
AFGHANISTAN
PAKISTAN
NEPAL
BHUTAN
TAIWAN
Tropic of Cancer

WESTERN SAHARA
ALGERIA
LIBYA
EGYPT
JORDAN
KUWAIT
BAHRAIN
Q
SAUDI ARABIA
UAE
OMAN
INDIA
MYANMAR

CAPE VERDE ISLANDS
MAURITANIA
MALI
NIGER
CHAD
SUDAN
ERITREA
YEMEN REPUBLIC
DJIBOUTI
Socotra
BANGLADESH
LAOS
NORTHERN MARIANAS
Pacific Ocean

SENEGAL
G
G-B
GUINEA
BU
BE
NIGERIA
CAR
ETHIOPIA
SOMALIA
THAILAND
VIETNAM
PHILIPPINES
GUAM
FEDERATED STATES OF MICRONESIA
MARSHALL ISLANDS

SIERRA LEONE
LIBERIA
COTE D'IVOIRE
GHANA
TOGO
CAMEROON
EQUATORIAL GUINEA
U
KENYA
SRI LANKA
MALDIVES
CAMBODIA
BD
MALAYSIA
SINGAPORE
Equator
KIRIBATI

GABON
CONGO
Cabinda
RWANDA
CONGO DEMOCRATIC REPUBLIC
BURUNDI
TANZANIA
SEYCHELLES
I N D O N E S I A
PAPUA NEW GUINEA
SOLOMON ISLANDS
NAURU
TUVALU

Atlantic Ocean
ANGOLA
MALAWI
COMOROS
ZAMBIA
Indian Ocean
VANUATU
FIJI

NAMIBIA
ZIM
MOZAMBIQUE
MADAGASCAR
MAURITIUS
Réunion
New Caledonia
AUSTRALIA
Tropic of Capricorn

BOTSWANA
SWAZILAND
REPUBLIC OF SOUTH AFRICA
LESOTHO

Kerguelen
NEW ZEALAND

Prime Meridian

Eckert IV Projection

Equator
Prime Meridian

Equator
Prime Meridian

© Oxford University Press

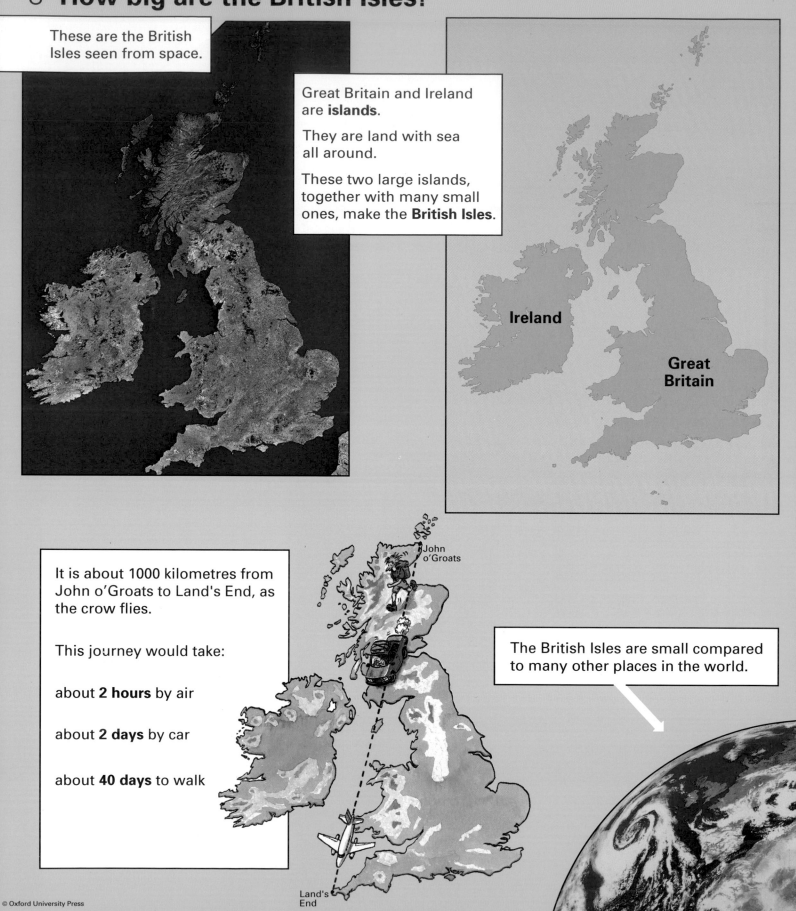

These are the British Isles seen from space.

Great Britain and Ireland are **islands**.

They are land with sea all around.

These two large islands, together with many small ones, make the **British Isles**.

Ireland

Great Britain

John o'Groats

It is about 1000 kilometres from John o'Groats to Land's End, as the crow flies.

This journey would take:

about **2 hours** by air

about **2 days** by car

about **40 days** to walk

The British Isles are small compared to many other places in the world.

Land's End

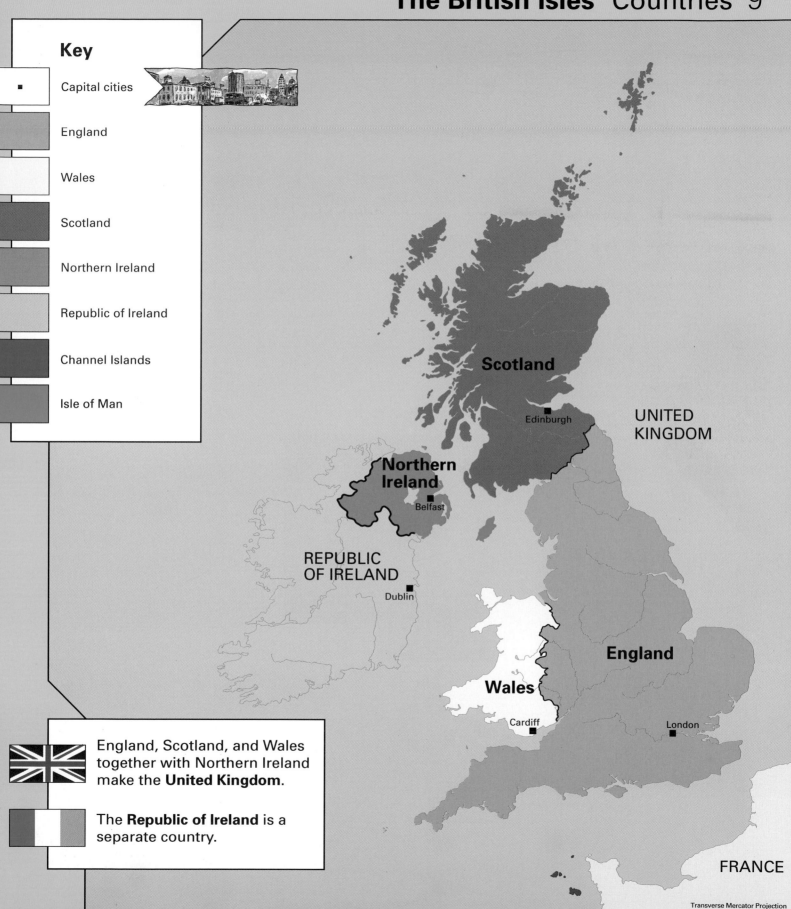

Key

- ▪ Capital cities
- England
- Wales
- Scotland
- Northern Ireland
- Republic of Ireland
- Channel Islands
- Isle of Man

England, Scotland, and Wales together with Northern Ireland make the **United Kingdom**.

The **Republic of Ireland** is a separate country.

Scotland

Edinburgh

UNITED KINGDOM

Northern Ireland

Belfast

REPUBLIC OF IRELAND

Dublin

England

Wales

Cardiff

London

FRANCE

Transverse Mercator Projection
© Oxford University Press

10 Rivers, hills, and mountains

highest peaks

from these you can
see a long way in all
directions

mountains

steep, rocky slopes

moors and uplands

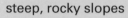

high, wind-swept
places with heather
and rough grass

hills

smooth slopes and
gentle valleys

low lands

mostly flat, marshy
land with wide rivers

rivers

rainwater runs downhill
to collect in rivers which
flow to the sea

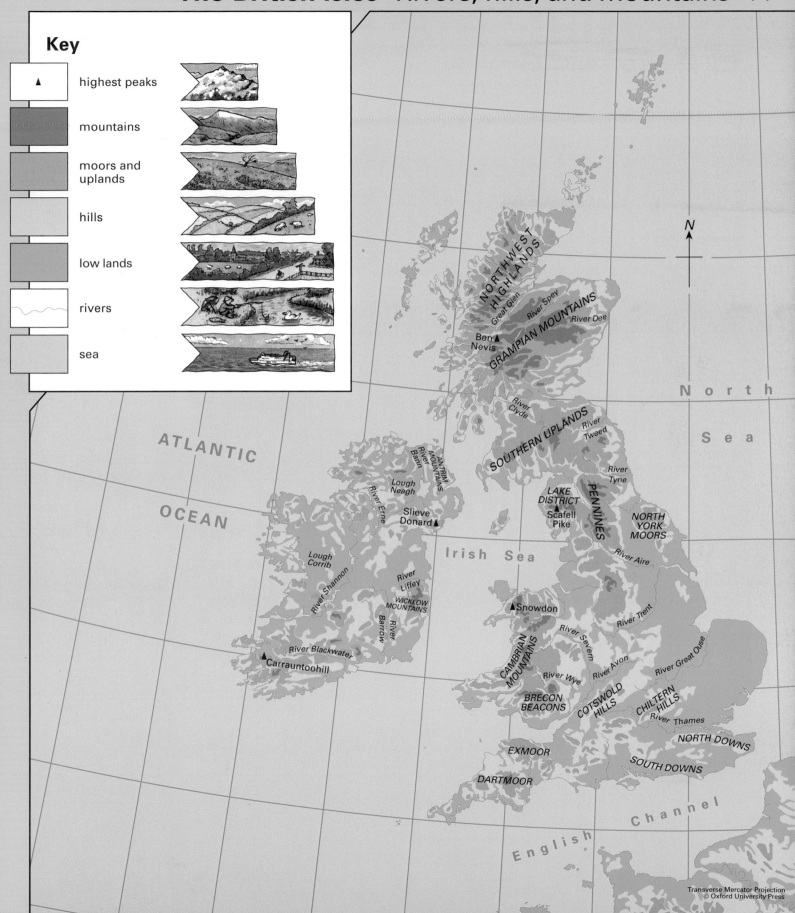

Key

▲ highest peaks

mountains

moors and uplands

hills

low lands

rivers

sea

NORTHWEST HIGHLANDS

Great Glen

River Spey

GRAMPIAN MOUNTAINS

River Dee

Ben Nevis ▲

River Clyde

SOUTHERN UPLANDS

River Tweed

River Tyne

ATLANTIC OCEAN

River Bann

ANTRIM MOUNTAINS

Lough Neagh

River Erne

Slieve Donard ▲

Irish Sea

LAKE DISTRICT

Scafell Pike ▲

PENNINES

NORTH YORK MOORS

River Aire

N o r t h   S e a

Lough Corrib

River Shannon

River Liffey

WICKLOW MOUNTAINS

River Barrow

River Blackwater

Carrauntoohill ▲

▲ Snowdon

River Trent

CAMBRIAN MOUNTAINS

River Severn

River Wye

River Avon

River Great Ouse

CHILTERN HILLS

BRECON BEACONS

COTSWOLD HILLS

River Thames

NORTH DOWNS

EXMOOR

SOUTH DOWNS

DARTMOOR

E n g l i s h   C h a n n e l

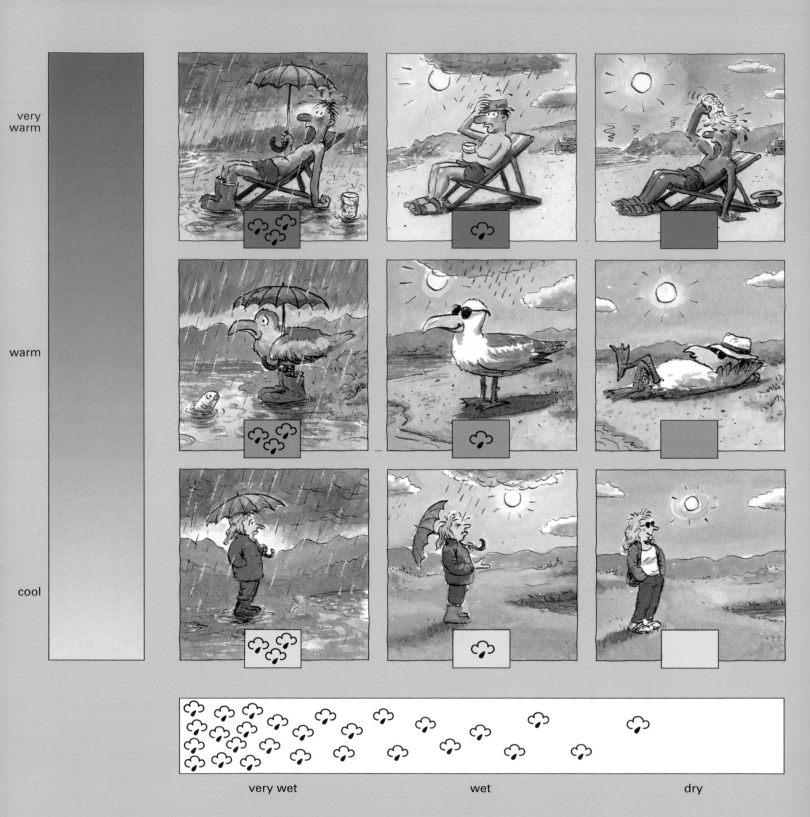

very warm

warm

cool

very wet

wet

dry

Legend:

very warm

warm

cool

very wet

wet

dry

The hottest places in Britain are Penzance in Cornwall and the Isles of Scilly.

The driest place in Britain is St Osyth, near Clacton-on-Sea, in Essex.

The strongest gust of wind ever recorded in Britain was at Cairn Gorm, Highland Region.

Cairn Gorm

St Osyth

Penzance

Isles of Scilly

Transverse Mercator Projection
© Oxford University Press

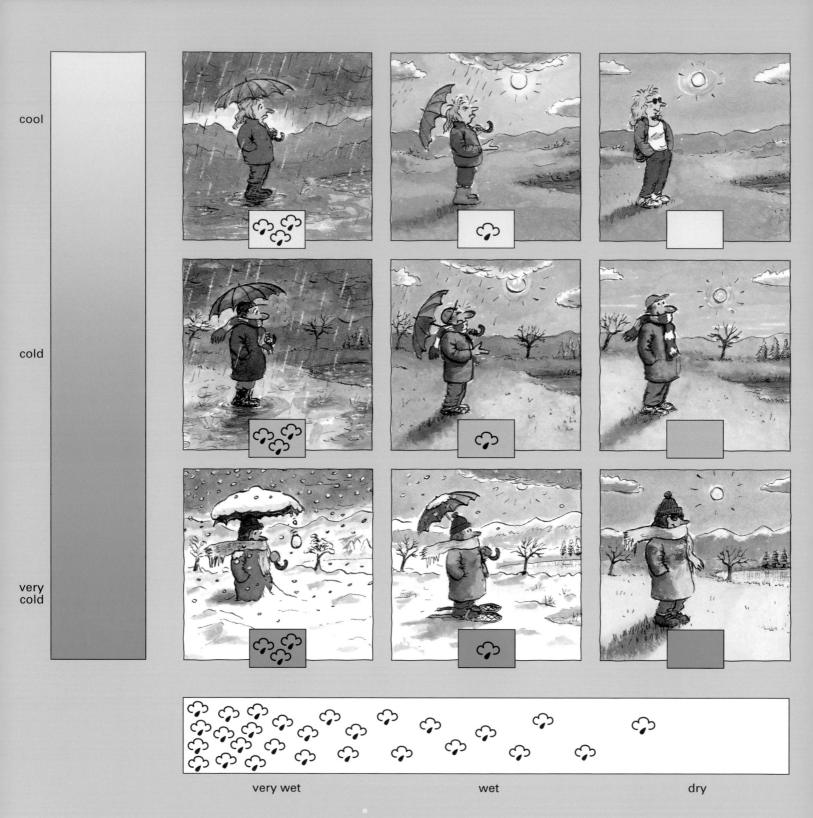

cool

cold

very
cold

very wet   wet   dry

Legend

- cool
- cold
- very cold
- very wet
- wet
- dry

The coldest place in Britain is Braemar, Grampian.

The wettest place in Britain is Sty Head Tarn, near Scafell Pike, in Cumbria.

The snowiest places in Britain are Upper Teesdale and the hills of North Wales near Denbigh.

Braemar

Upper Teesdale

Sty Head Tarn ▲

Denbighshire Hills

Transverse Mercator Projection
© Oxford University Press

16 A picture from space

Pictures from space show lots of detail but it is hard to see each town and road.

Maps pick out the most important places and show their names.

Key

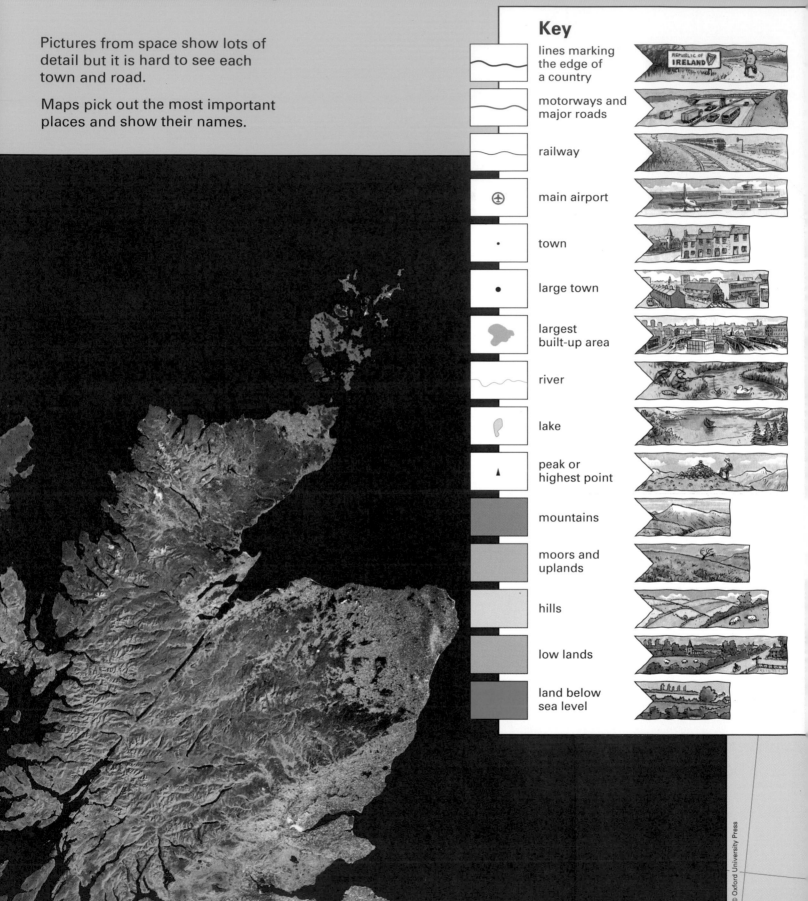

lines marking the edge of a country	
motorways and major roads	
railway	
main airport	
town	
large town	
largest built-up area	
river	
lake	
peak or highest point	
mountains	
moors and uplands	
hills	
low lands	
land below sea level	

Transverse Mercator Projection
© Oxford University Press

B   **C**   **D**   **E**   **F**   **G**   **H**   **J**

5

N

Shetland
Islands

Herma
Ness

Unst

Fetlar

Yell

Out
Skerries

Whalsay

Mainland

Bressay

Foula

Scalloway

Lerwick

5

A

Sumburgh
Head

4

A T L A N T I C

O C E A N

Fair
Isle

4

Rona

Papa
Westray

North
Ronaldsay

Westray
Rousay

Sanday

Orkney
Islands

Eday

Stronsay

Mainland

Shapinsay

Stromness

Kirkwall

3

Hoy

South
Ronaldsay

Butt of Lewis

Cape Wrath

Pentland Firth'

Duncansby Head
John o' Groats

3

Thurso

Stornoway
Lewis

River Thurso

Wick

N
o
r
t
h

Clisham
799m

Ben More
Assynt
998m

NORTHWEST HIGHLANDS

Loch Shin

2

St
Kilda

Harris
Scalpay

Ullapool

Dornoch Firth

S
e
a

Outer Hebrides

The Minch

Pabbay

Berneray

North
Uist

Little Minch

Sgurr Mor
1109m

Tarbat Ness

Ben Wyvis
1046m

Moray Firth

Fraserburgh

2

Benbecula

Portree
Raasay

Skye
CUILLIN
HILLS
1009m

Dingwall

Inverness

Elgin

Peterhead

South
Uist

Kyle of
Lochalsh

Carn Eige
1183m

Loch
Ness

River Spey

River Deveron

Barra

Canna

Aviemore

CAIRNGORMS

River Don

Aberdeen

Mingulay

Rhum

Eigg

Fort Augustus

MONADHLIATH
MOUNTAINS

Ben Macdui
1310m

River Dee

Mallaig

Great Glen

Braemar

River North Esk

1

Coll

Ben Nevis
1344m

GRAMPIAN MOUNTAINS

River South Esk

Montrose

Tiree

Fort
William

Forfar

Ulva

Mull

Ben
Cruachan
1126m

Loch
Rannoch

Loch Tay

River Tay

SIDLAW HILLS

Arbroath

1

Iona

Loch Linnhe

S C O T L A N D

Oban

Perth

Dundee

Colonsay

Jura

Loch
Awe

Loch Fyne

St Andrews

Glenrothes

Firth of Lorn

Loch
Lomond

River Forth

Stirling

Kirkcaldy

Inner Hebrides

Sound of Sleat

Firth of Forth

B   **C**   **D**   **E**   **F**   **G**   **H**

Key

- lines marking the edge of a country
- motorways and major roads
- railway
- ⊕ main airport
- · town
- • large town
- largest built-up area
- river
- lake
- ▲ peak or highest point
- mountains
- moors and uplands
- hills
- low lands
- land below sea level

Transverse Mercator Projection
© Oxford University Press

© Oxford University Press

A map of Wales and surrounding regions.

Grid references (top): A B C D E F G H
Grid references (side): 6 5 4 3 2

Seas and water bodies:
Irish Sea
ATLANTIC OCEAN
St George's Channel
Bristol Channel
Cardigan Bay
Lyme Bay
English Channel

Republic of Ireland labels:
Lough Ree, Athlone, Navan, Mullingar, R. Boyne, Tullamore, R. Liffey, Swords, Dublin, Dún Laoghaire, Bray, Naas, Kildare, Portlaoise, R. Barrow, REPUBLIC OF IRELAND, R. Shannon, Lough Derg, Birr, Roscrea, Nenagh, R. Nore, Carlow, R. Slaney, Tullow, Wicklow, SILVERMINE MOUNTAINS, Kilkenny, Thurles, Cashel, Tipperary, Cahir, R. Suir, Clonmel, Carrick-on-Suir, Galtymore 920m, Waterford, Dungarvan, Youghal, New Ross, Wexford, Rosslare, Enniscorthy, Gorey, Arklow, WICKLOW MOUNTAINS, Lugnaquilia 926m, Carnsore Point

Wales labels:
WALES, CAMBRIAN MOUNTAINS, Holyhead, Anglesey, Amlwch, Llandudno, Conwy, Colwyn Bay, Bangor, Caernarfon, Snowdon 1085m, Denbigh, Wrexham, Llangollen, Pwllheli, Dolgellau, Barmouth, Cader Idris 892m, Aberystwyth, New Quay, Cardigan, St David's Head, Fishguard, Carmarthen, R. Teifi, Llandovery, R. Tywi, Milford Haven, Llanelli, Neath, Swansea, Port Talbot, Merthyr Tydfil, Rhondda, Caerphilly, Bridgend, Barry, Brecon, BRECON BEACONS, BLACK MOUNTAINS, Pontypool, Cwmbran, Newport, Cardiff, R. Dovey, R. Severn, Newtown, R. Wye, Hay-on-Wye, R. Usk, Monmouth

England labels:
Chorley, Southport, Rochdale, Bolton, Bury, Oldham, Huddersfield, Liverpool, Birkenhead, Wigan, Warrington, Manchester, Doncaster, Rotherham, Stockport, Sheffield, Widnes, Runcorn, Buxton, Works, Chester, Macclesfield, Chester, Crewe, River Dee, Oswestry, Stoke-on-Trent, Matlock, Stafford, Burton upon Trent, Derby, Long, Ilkeston, River Vyrnwy, Shrewsbury, Telford, Cannock, Coalville, Wolverhampton, Walsall, Bridgnorth, West Bromwich, Dudley, Birmingham, Kidderminster, Solihull, Coventry, R. Teme, Redditch, Rugby, Worcester, R. Avon, Warwick, Great Malvern, Hereford, Evesham, Stratford-upon-Avon, Banbury, Cheltenham, HILLS, Gloucester, R. Severn, R. Cherwell, Stroud, COTSWOLD, Cirencester, HILLS, Oxford, R. Thames, Bristol, Swindon, Weston-super-Mare, Bath, MENDIP HILLS, Trowbridge, Newbury, Basingstoke, Lundy, Ilfracombe, Minehead, Bridgwater, QUANTOCK HILLS, SALISBURY PLAIN, Hartland Point, EXMOOR, R. Exe, Salisbury, Winchester, Barnstaple, R. Taw, Taunton, R. Parrett, R. Yeo, Yeovil, R. Stour, Eastleigh, Tiverton, Southampton, Fareham, Trevose Head, Yes Tor 619m, DARTMOOR, River Teign, Exeter, Lyme Regis, Dorchester, R. Frome, Weymouth, Poole, Portsmouth, BODMIN MOOR, River Tamar, R. Dart, Exmouth, Portland Bill, Bournemouth, Isle of Wight, Newquay, Torbay, Dartmouth, Swanage, St Ives, Truro, St Austell, Plymouth, Start Point, Penzance, Land's End, Falmouth, Lizard Point, Isles of Scilly

Channel Islands and France labels:
Alderney, Cap de la Hague, Channel Islands, St Peter-Port, Cherbourg, Valognes, Guernsey, Sark, Jersey, St Helier, Carentan, Coutances

N (compass)

Key

~~	lines marking the edge of a country
~~	motorways and major roads
~~	railway
⊕	main airport
·	town
•	large town
▮	largest built-up area
~~	river
⬧	lake
▲	peak or highest point
▮	mountains
▮	moors and uplands
▮	hills
▮	low lands
▮	land below sea level

REPUBLIC OF IRELAND

J K L M N 6

River Trent
Scunthorpe
Spurn Head
Grimsby
erham
Louth
Mablethorpe
op
Lincoln
LINCOLN WOLDS
rfield
Skegness
Newark-on-Trent
Wells-next-the-Sea
Nottingham
Boston
The Wash
Cromer
Eaton
Grantham
Spalding
King's Lynn
River Bure
ughborough
R. Welland
THE FENS
Wisbech
River Wensum
Leicester
R. Nene
Norwich
Great Yarmouth
Corby
Peterborough
Thetford
Lowestoft
Kettering
R. Great Ouse
Ely
River Waveney
Southwold
Northampton
Bury St Edmunds
Southwold
Cambridge
Aldeburgh
Bedford
E N G L A N D
Milton Keynes
River Stour
Ipswich
HILLS
Felixstowe
Luton
Harwich
Aylesbury
Welwyn Garden City
Colchester
CHILTERN
Harlow
St Osyth
St Albans
Chelmsford
Watford
R. Lea
Basildon
Slough
Southend-on-sea
Windsor
London
Gravesend
Margate
Reading
Sheerness
Woking
Gillingham
Canterbury
Reigate
NORTH
Deal
Guildford
Redhill
Maidstone
DOWNS
Dover
Crawley
R. Medway
Ashford
Horsham
THE
Royal
Folkestone
R. Arun
WEALD
Tunbridge Wells
SOUTH
DOWNS
Hastings
Havant
Brighton
Eastbourne
Bognor Regis
Worthing
Beachy Head
Newhaven

North Sea

5

4

Ostend
Nieuwpoort
Dunkerque
BELGIUM
Calais
Poperinge
Strait of Dover
Cassel
St-Omer
Armentières
Boulogne-sur-Mer
Lillers
3
Montreuil-sur-Mer
Bruay-en-Artois
Lens
le Touquet-Paris-Plage
Hesdin
Arras
Berck-Plage
E
Doullens
le Tréport
Abbeville
River Somme
Dieppe
St Valery-en-Caux
Blangy-sur-Bresle
Amiens
St Quentin
Fécamp
Neufchâtel-en-Bray
Poix-de-Picardie
Roye
Etretat
N
Montdidier
Laon
Baie de la Seine
Bolbec
Yvetot
Forges-les-Eaux
Noyon
2
le Havre
Gournay-en-Bray
Compiègne
Honfleur
Pont-Audemer
Beauvais
Soissons
Deauville-les-Bains
A
Rouen
Clermont
Oise
Bayeux
R
Gisors
River Seine
Cabourg
F
Louviers
Senlis
Château-Thierry
J Caen
Lisieux
K Evreux
Vernon
L
Paris M
Meaux N

Transverse Mercator Projection
© Oxford University Press

Large towns and built-up areas have lots of houses, schools, shops, offices, and factories.

This photograph shows part of Leicester.

Most people in Britain live and work
in large towns and built-up areas.

Key

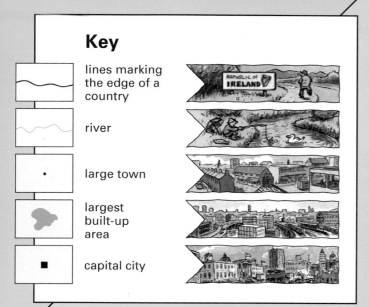

	lines marking the edge of a country
	river
·	large town
	largest built-up area
■	capital city

Aberdeen

Scotland

Glasgow ■ **Edinburgh**

Northern Ireland

Newcastle upon Tyne

Sunderland

■ **Belfast**

UNITED KINGDOM

REPUBLIC OF IRELAND

Leeds
Bradford Kingston upon Hull
Liverpool Manchester
Sheffield
Stoke-on-Trent
Nottingham
Derby
Wolverhampton Leicester Norwich
Birmingham
Coventry

Wales **England**

■ **Cardiff** ■ **London**

Bristol

Southampton

Plymouth

FRANCE

farmland

farmers use the land to produce food by growing crops and keeping animals

forest

forest land is used to grow trees for timber

coast

much land at the edge of the sea is used for holidays

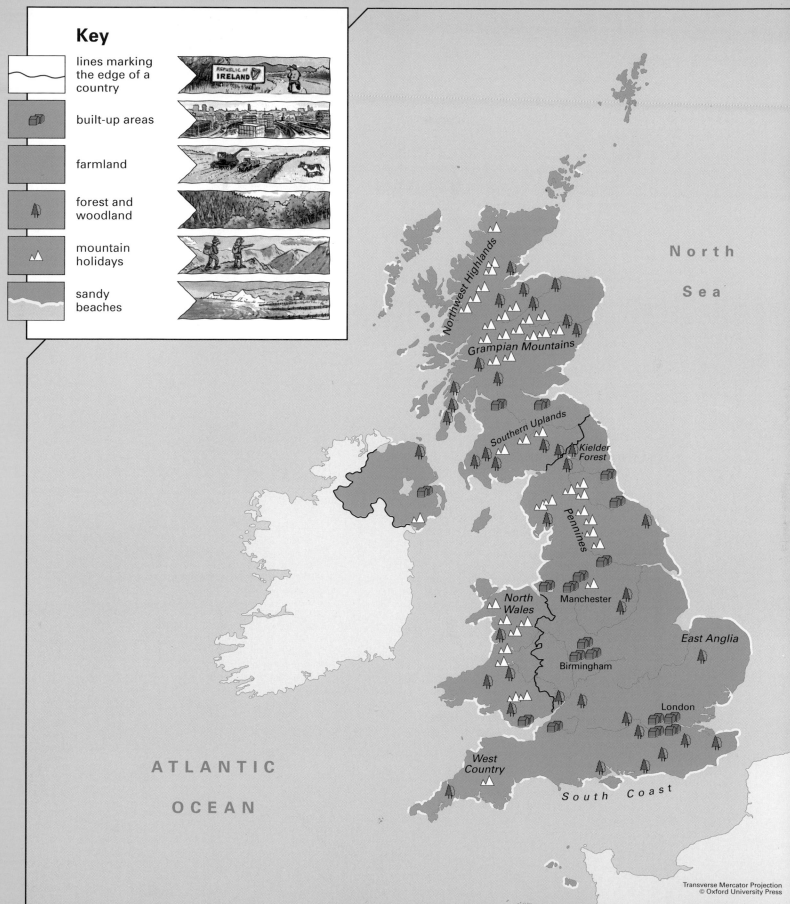

Key

lines marking the edge of a country	
built-up areas	
farmland	
forest and woodland	
mountain holidays	
sandy beaches	

REPUBLIC OF IRELAND

North Sea

Northwest Highlands

Grampian Mountains

Southern Uplands

Kielder Forest

Pennines

North Wales

Manchester

East Anglia

Birmingham

London

West Country

South Coast

ATLANTIC

OCEAN

Transverse Mercator Projection
© Oxford University Press

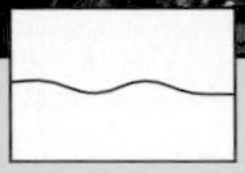

railway

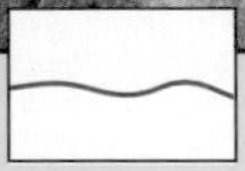

motorway

airport

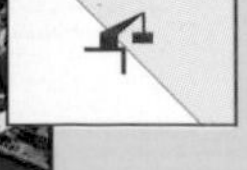

port

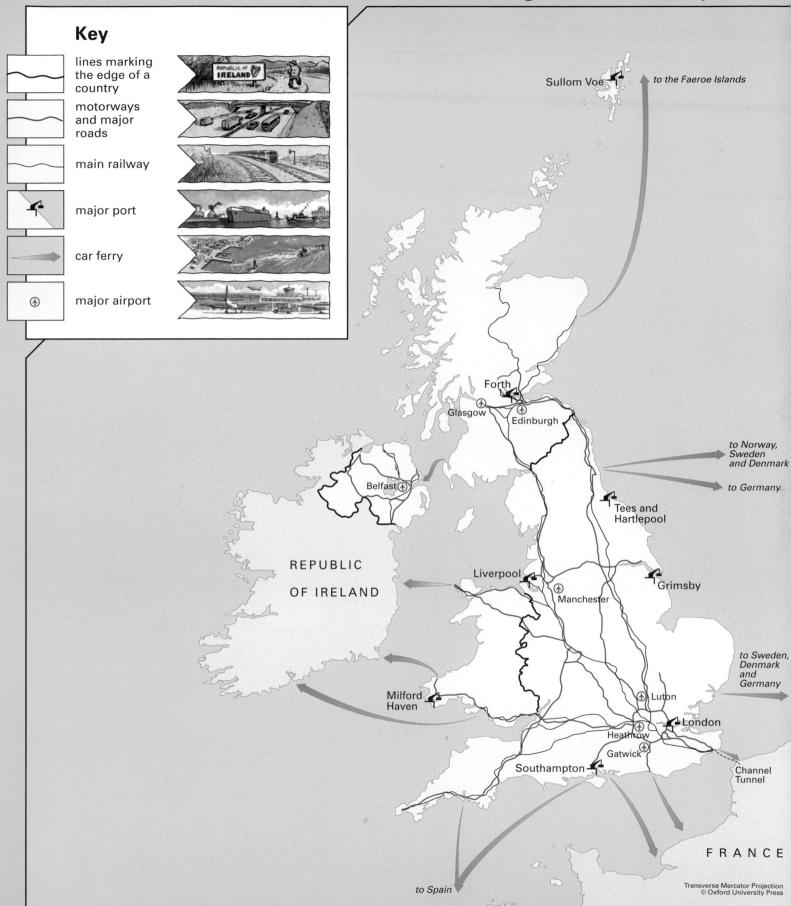

Key

lines marking the edge of a country

motorways and major roads

main railway

major port

car ferry

major airport

Sullom Voe

to the Faeroe Islands

Forth

Glasgow

Edinburgh

to Norway, Sweden and Denmark

to Germany

Belfast

Tees and Hartlepool

REPUBLIC

OF IRELAND

Liverpool

Grimsby

Manchester

Milford Haven

to Sweden, Denmark and Germany

Luton

London

Heathrow

Channel Tunnel

Gatwick

Southampton

to Spain

FRANCE

mountains

desert

savannah

marsh

hot forest

cold forest

The photographs show different environments.
They are our natural surroundings.

The matching symbols are used on the maps on pages 30-39.

 ice and icebergs

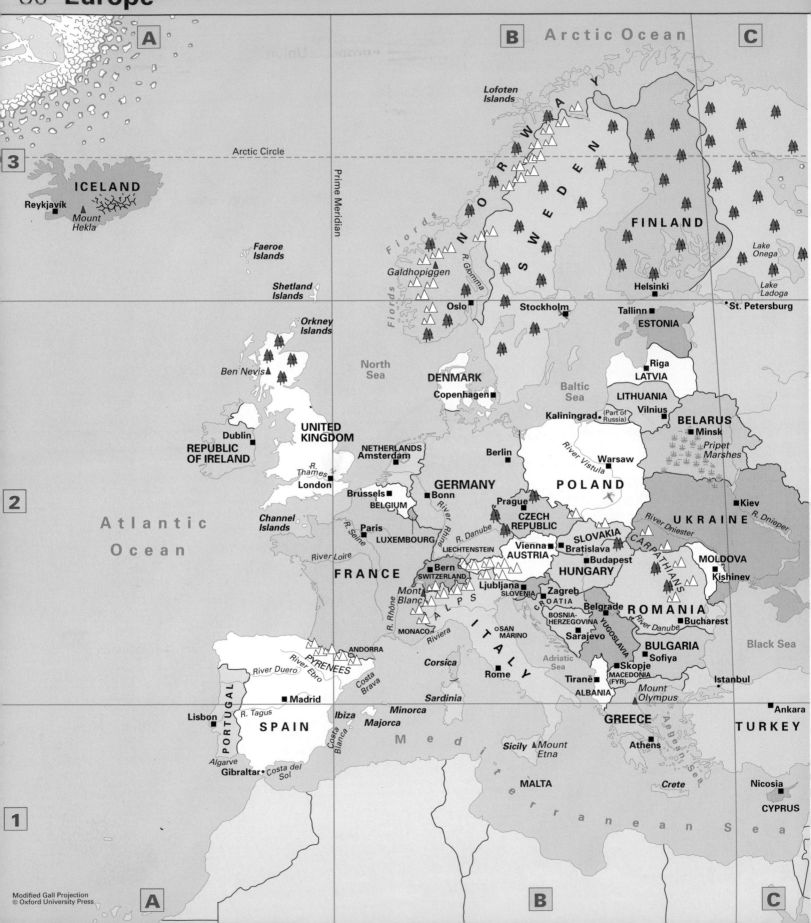

Arctic Ocean

A

B

C

Lofoten
Islands

Arctic Circle

ICELAND

Reykjavík ■

Mount
Hekla ▲

3

Prime Meridian

Faeroe
Islands

Shetland
Islands

Orkney
Islands

Ben Nevis ▲

North
Sea

DENMARK

Copenhagen ■

Dublin ■

**REPUBLIC
OF IRELAND**

**UNITED
KINGDOM**

R.
Thames

London ■

NETHERLANDS
Amsterdam ■

Brussels ■
BELGIUM

Bonn ■

Berlin ■

GERMANY

Channel
Islands

R. Seine

Paris ■

LUXEMBOURG

R. Rhine

Prague ■

**CZECH
REPUBLIC**

River Vistula

Warsaw ■

POLAND

LIECHTENSTEIN

FRANCE

Bern ■
SWITZERLAND

R. Danube

Vienna ■
AUSTRIA

Bratislava ■

Budapest ■

HUNGARY

River Loire

R. Rhône

Mont
Blanc

ALPS

Ljubljana ■
SLOVENIA

Zagreb ■

CROATIA

**Atlantic
Ocean**

NORWAY

SWEDEN

Galdhøpiggen

Oslo ■

R. Glomma

Stockholm ■

FINLAND

Helsinki ■

Lake
Onega

Lake
Ladoga

Tallinn ■

ESTONIA

Riga ■

LATVIA

LITHUANIA

Kaliningrad ■

Vilnius ■

(Part of
Russia)

BELARUS

Minsk ■

Pripet
Marshes

Kiev ■

R. Dnieper

UKRAINE

River Dniester

CARPATHIANS

MOLDOVA

Kishinev ■

Belgrade ■

ROMANIA

Bucharest ■

St. Petersburg

Baltic
Sea

MONACO ■

Riviera

PORTUGAL

Lisbon ■

R. Tagus

SPAIN

Madrid ■

River Duero

River Ebro

PYRENEES

ANDORRA

Costa
Brava

Corsica

Sardinia

ITALY

**SAN
MARINO**

Rome ■

**BOSNIA-
HERZEGOVINA**

Sarajevo ■

YUGOSLAVIA

River Danube

BULGARIA

Sofiya ■

Skopje ■
**MACEDONIA
(FYR)**

Tiranë ■

ALBANIA

Mount
Olympus ▲

Adriatic
Sea

Black Sea

Istanbul ■

Ankara ■

TURKEY

Ibiza

Minorca

Majorca

GREECE

Athens ■

Aegean
Sea

Algarve

Gibraltar ■

Costa del
Sol

Costa
Blanca

M e d

Sicily ▲Mount
Etna

MALTA

Crete

Nicosia ■

CYPRUS

i t e r r a n e a n S e a

2

1

Fjords

Fjords

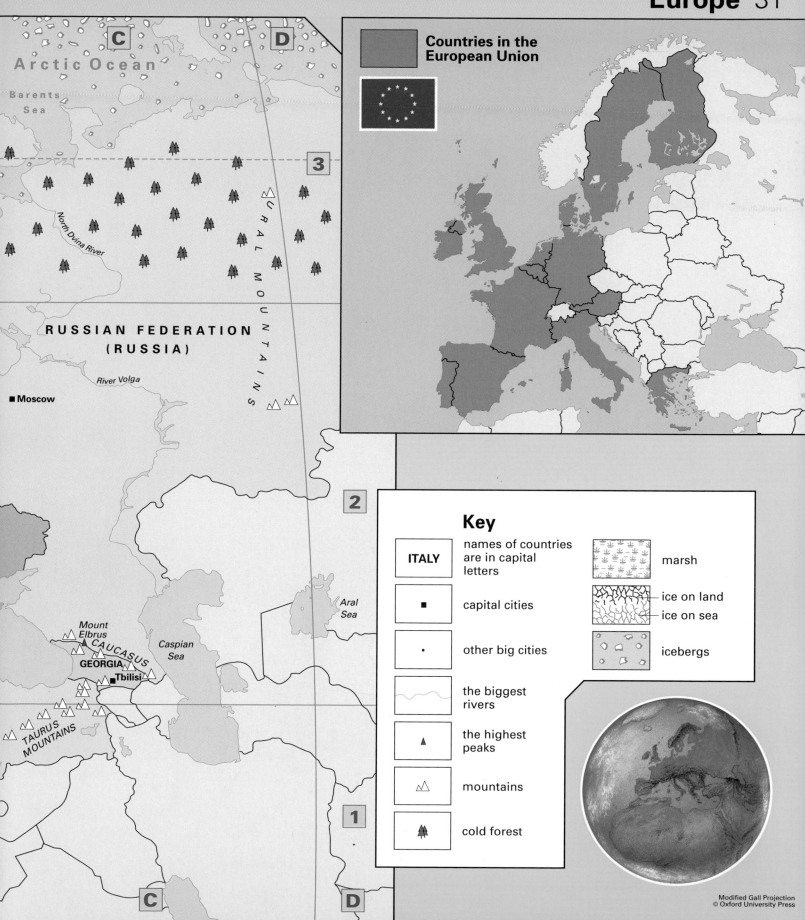

Arctic Ocean

Barents Sea

North Dvina River

URAL MOUNTAINS

RUSSIAN FEDERATION (RUSSIA)

River Volga

■ Moscow

Aral Sea

Mount Elbrus

CAUCASUS

GEORGIA

■ Tbilisi

Caspian Sea

TAURUS MOUNTAINS

Countries in the European Union

Key

ITALY	names of countries are in capital letters	
■	capital cities	
•	other big cities	
	the biggest rivers	
▲	the highest peaks	
⋀	mountains	
🌲	cold forest	

marsh

ice on land
ice on sea

icebergs

Modified Gall Projection
© Oxford University Press

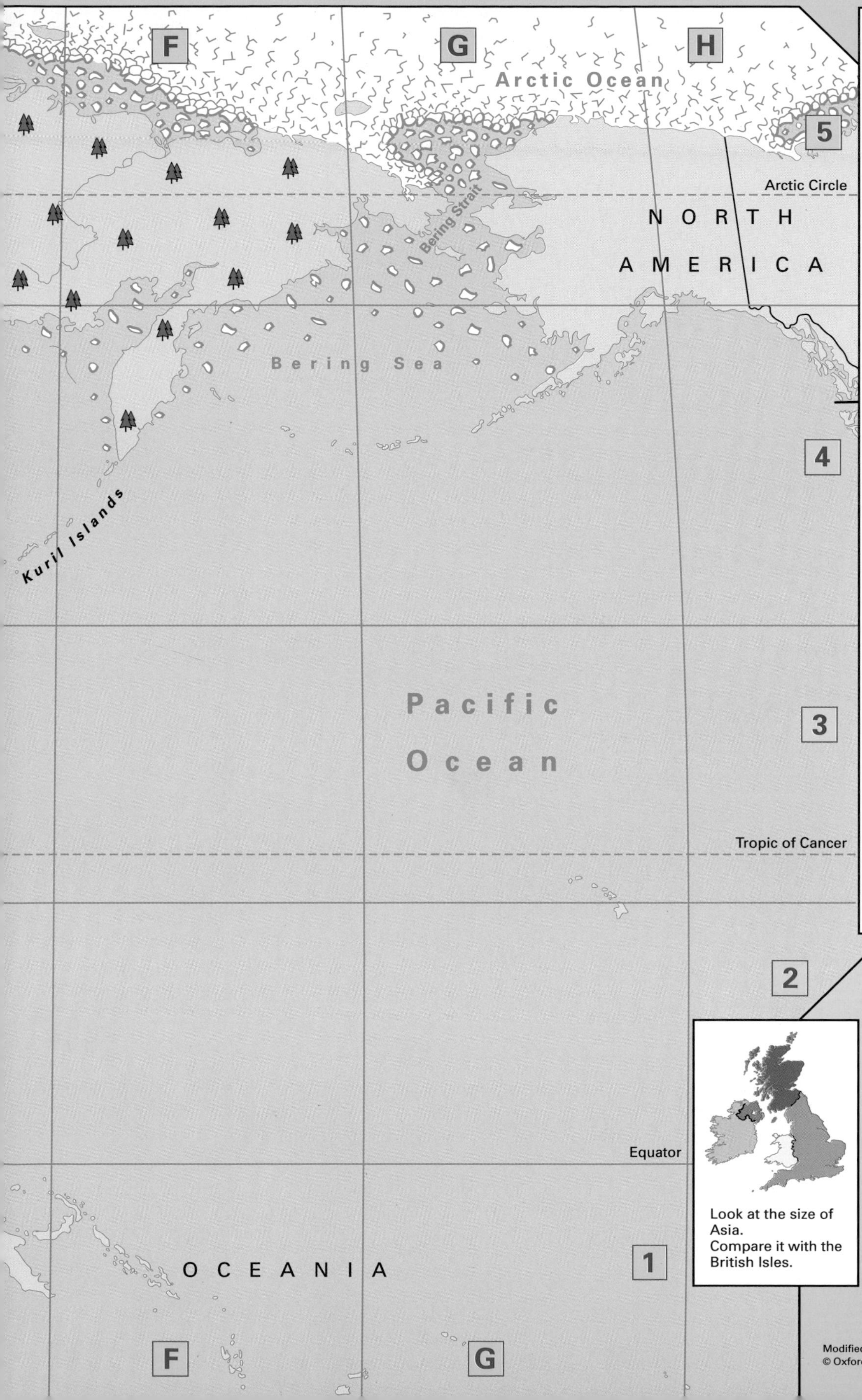

F G H

Arctic Ocean

Arctic Circle

5

N O R T H

A M E R I C A

Bering Strait

Bering Sea

Kuril Islands

4

P a c i f i c

O c e a n

3

Tropic of Cancer

2

Equator

Look at the size of
Asia.
Compare it with the
British Isles.

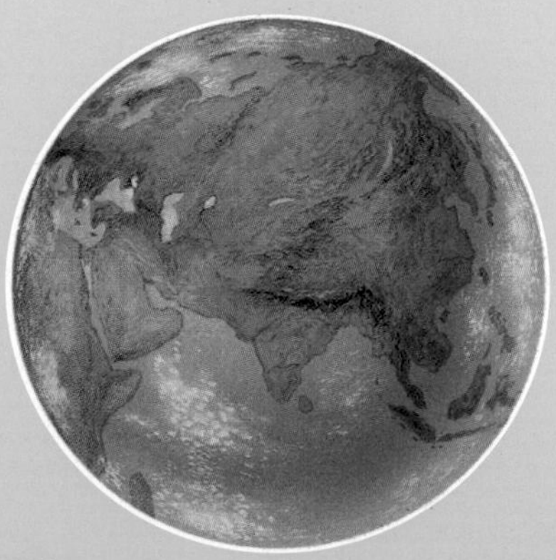

1

O C E A N I A

F G

Key

CHINA	names of countries are in capital letters
■	capital cities
·	other big cities
～	the biggest rivers
▲	the highest peaks
⩕	mountains
🌲	cold forest
	desert
🌳	hot forest
	marsh
	ice on land
	ice on sea
	icebergs

Modified Gall Projection
© Oxford University Press

A · Arctic Ocean · B · C · D

Baffin Bay

5 · Alaska · Baffin Island · **5**
Arctic Circle

Bering Strait

Mount McKinley · Mount Logan · C · A · N · A · D · A

Bering Sea · Hudson Bay · LABRADOR

Aleutian Islands · **4** · R · O · C · K · Y · M · O · U · N · T · A · I · N · S · Newfoundland · **4**

St Lawrence River

Great Lakes · Montréal
Ottawa · Toronto
Detroit · Boston
Chicago · New York
San Francisco · Philadelphia · Washington D.C.

Mount Whitney · UNITED · STATES · OF · AMERICA · APPALACHIANS

Los Angeles · Dallas · Bermuda

3 · Pacific · Rio Grande · Houston · River Mississippi · Atlantic · **3**
Ocean · Ocean · River Missouri

Gulf of Mexico · Miami · THE BAHAMAS · Tropic of Cancer

Hawaiian Islands · MEXICO · CUBA · DOMINICAN REPUBLIC
Citlaltépetl · JAMAICA · HAITI · ANTIGUA AND BARBUDA
BELIZE · PUERTO RICO · DOMINICA
HONDURAS · Caribbean Sea · ST LUCIA
GUATEMALA · BARBADOS
EL SALVADOR · NICARAGUA · ST VINCENT AND THE GRENADINES

2 · COSTA RICA · TRINIDAD AND TOBAGO · **2**
PANAMA

Equator

A · B · C · D · E
1 · **1**

Modified Gall Projection
© Oxford University Press

Key

CUBA	names of countries are in capital letters
■	capital cities
•	other big cities
～	the biggest rivers
▲	the highest peaks
△△	mountains
🌲	cold forest
	desert
⥁	savannah
🌳	hot forest
	marsh
	ice on land
	ice on sea
	icebergs

Look at the size of North America and the size of South America. Compare them with the British Isles.

Modified Gall Projection
© Oxford University Press

Tropic of Cancer

Atlantic Ocean

Caracas
VENEZUELA
River Orinoco
Georgetown
Paramaribo
GUYANA
Cayenne
Bogotá
SURINAME
COLOMBIA
FRENCH GUIANA

Equator

Quito
ECUADOR
Cotopaxi
Galapagos Islands
Chimborazo
ANDES
River Amazon

BRAZIL

PERU
Lima
ANDES
Lake Titicaca
La Paz
Brasília
BOLIVIA
River Paraguay
River Paraná
Rio de Janeiro

Tropic of Capricorn
Pacific Ocean
PARAGUAY
São Paulo
Asunción

ATACAMA DESERT
Mount Aconcagua
ANDES
URUGUAY

Juan Fernandez Islands
Santiago
Buenos Aires
Montevideo

CHILE
ARGENTINA

Atlantic Ocean

Stanley
Falkland Islands

Southern Ocean
Cape Horn

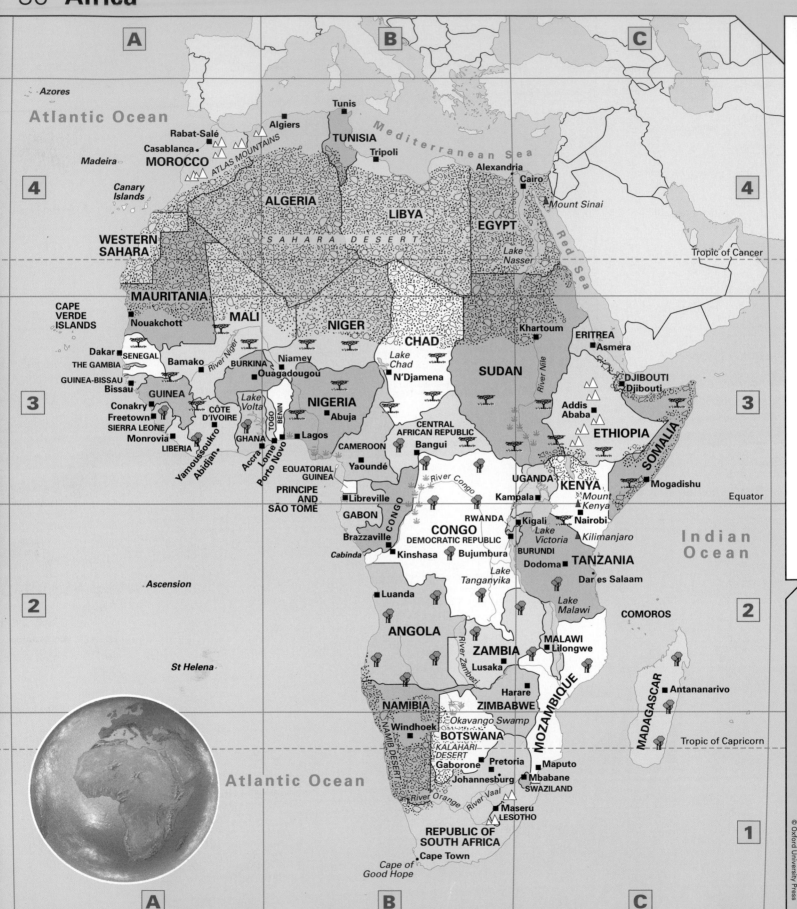

Azores

Atlantic Ocean

Rabat-Salé
Casablanca
MOROCCO
ATLAS MOUNTAINS
Madeira

Canary
Islands

Algiers
Tunis
TUNISIA
Tripoli
Mediterranean Sea
Alexandria
Cairo
Mount Sinai

ALGERIA
LIBYA
EGYPT

WESTERN
SAHARA

SAHARA DESERT

Lake
Nasser

Red Sea

Tropic of Cancer

CAPE
VERDE
ISLANDS

MAURITANIA
Nouakchott

MALI

NIGER

CHAD
Lake
Chad
N'Djamena

Khartoum

ERITREA
Asmera

Bamako
River Niger
BURKINA
Ouagadougou
Niamey

SUDAN
River Nile

Dakar
SENEGAL
THE GAMBIA
GUINEA-BISSAU
Bissau
GUINEA
Conakry
Freetown
SIERRA LEONE
Monrovia
LIBERIA
Yamoussoukro
Abidjan
CÔTE
D'IVOIRE
GHANA
Accra
Lomé
TOGO
BENIN
Porto Novo
Lake
Volta

NIGERIA
Abuja
Lagos

CENTRAL
AFRICAN REPUBLIC
Bangui

DJIBOUTI
Djibouti
Addis
Ababa
ETHIOPIA
SOMALIA

CAMEROON
Yaoundé
EQUATORIAL
GUINEA
PRINCIPE
AND
SÃO TOMÉ
GABON
Libreville
Brazzaville
Cabinda
Kinshasa

River Congo
CONGO
CONGO
DEMOCRATIC
REPUBLIC
RWANDA
Kigali
BURUNDI
Bujumbura

UGANDA
Kampala
Lake
Victoria
KENYA
Mount
Kenya
Nairobi
Kilimanjaro

Mogadishu

Equator

Ascension

Luanda

Lake
Tanganyika
Dodoma
TANZANIA
Dar es Salaam

Indian
Ocean

St Helena

ANGOLA
River Zambezi
ZAMBIA
Lusaka

Lake
Malawi
MALAWI
Lilongwe

COMOROS

MADAGASCAR
Antananarivo

NAMIBIA
NAMIB DESERT
Windhoek
BOTSWANA
KALAHARI
DESERT
Gaborone
Okavango Swamp
Harare
ZIMBABWE
MOZAMBIQUE

Tropic of Capricorn

Atlantic Ocean

Pretoria
Johannesburg
Maputo
Mbabane
SWAZILAND
River Orange
River Vaal
Maseru
LESOTHO
REPUBLIC OF
SOUTH AFRICA
Cape Town
Cape of
Good Hope

Modified Gall Projection
© Oxford University Press

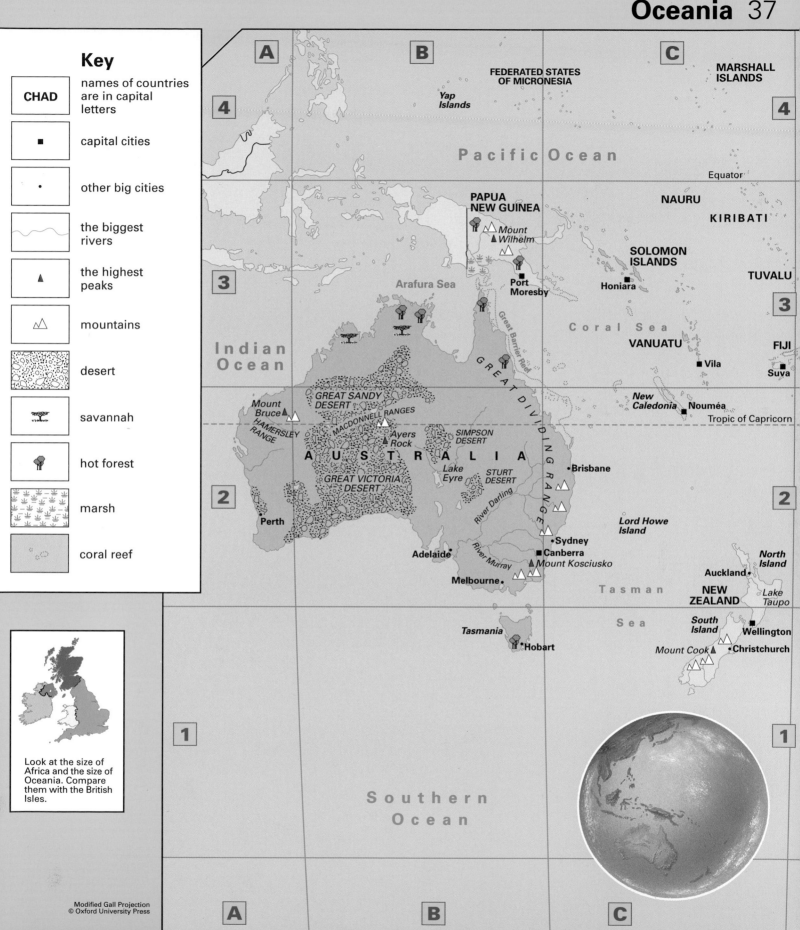

Key

CHAD	names of countries are in capital letters
■	capital cities
•	other big cities
~~	the biggest rivers
▲	the highest peaks
⋀⋀	mountains
	desert
	savannah
🌳	hot forest
	marsh
	coral reef

Look at the size of Africa and the size of Oceania. Compare them with the British Isles.

MARSHALL ISLANDS

FEDERATED STATES OF MICRONESIA

Yap Islands

Pacific Ocean

Equator

PAPUA NEW GUINEA

Mount Wilhelm

Port Moresby

NAURU

KIRIBATI

SOLOMON ISLANDS

Honiara

TUVALU

Arafura Sea

Indian Ocean

Coral Sea

VANUATU

FIJI

Vila

Suva

GREAT DIVIDING RANGE

Great Barrier Reef

New Caledonia

Nouméa

Tropic of Capricorn

Mount Bruce

HAMERSLEY RANGE

GREAT SANDY DESERT

MACDONNELL RANGES

Ayers Rock

SIMPSON DESERT

AUSTRALIA

Lake Eyre

STURT DESERT

Brisbane

GREAT VICTORIA DESERT

River Darling

Lord Howe Island

Perth

River Murray

Sydney

Adelaide

Canberra

Mount Kosciusko

Melbourne

North Island

Auckland

NEW ZEALAND

Lake Taupo

Tasman

Sea

South Island

Wellington

Tasmania

Mount Cook

Christchurch

Hobart

Southern Ocean

Modified Gall Projection
© Oxford University Press

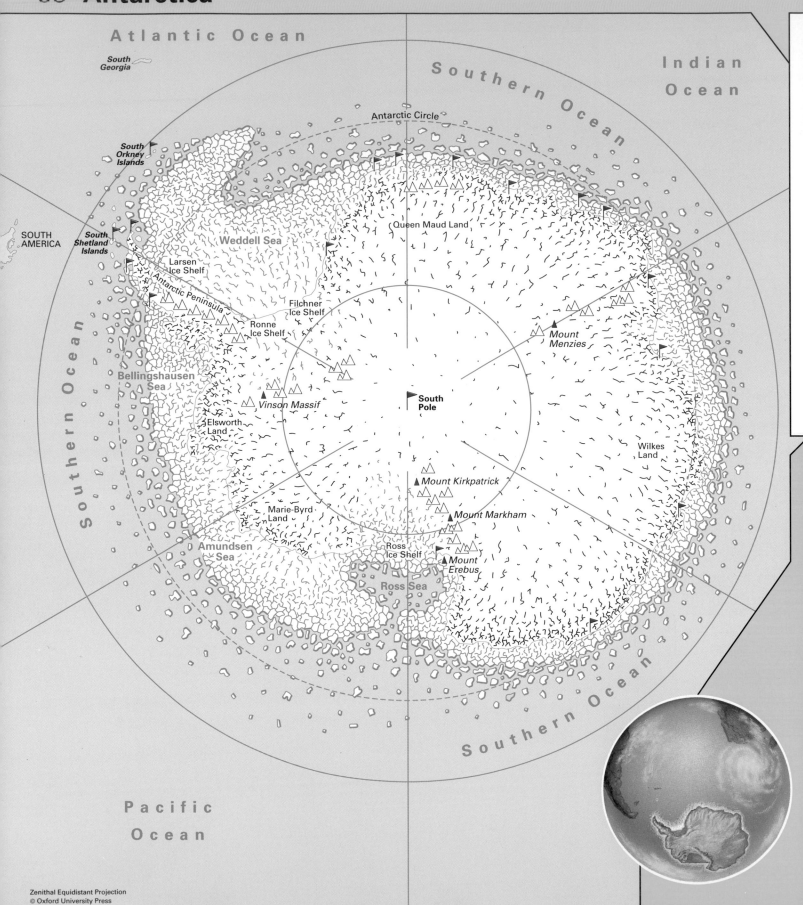

Atlantic Ocean

Indian Ocean

South Georgia

Southern Ocean

Antarctic Circle

South Orkney Islands

SOUTH AMERICA

South Shetland Islands

Queen Maud Land

Weddell Sea

Larsen Ice Shelf

Antarctic Peninsula

Filchner Ice Shelf

Ronne Ice Shelf

▲ Mount Menzies

Southern Ocean

Bellingshausen Sea

Vinson Massif

South Pole

Elsworth Land

Wilkes Land

Mount Kirkpatrick

Marie-Byrd Land

▲ Mount Markham

Amundsen Sea

Ross Ice Shelf

▲ Mount Erebus

Ross Sea

Southern Ocean

Pacific Ocean

Southern Ocean

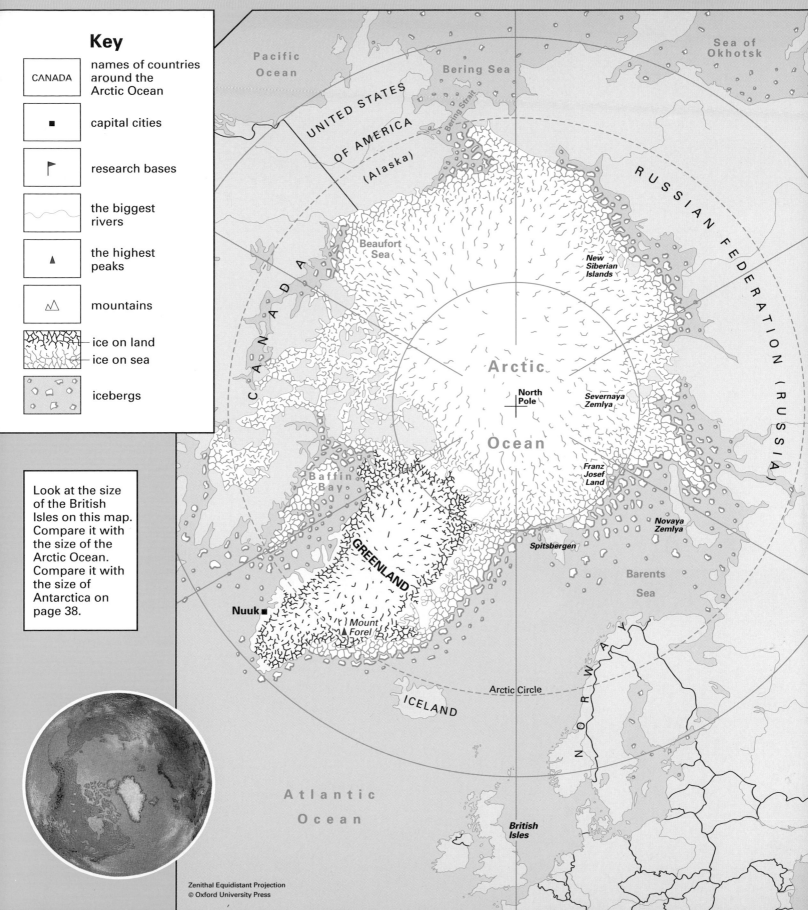

Key

CANADA	names of countries around the Arctic Ocean
■	capital cities
⚑	research bases
〰	the biggest rivers
▲	the highest peaks
△△	mountains
▨	ice on land / ice on sea
◌	icebergs

Look at the size of the British Isles on this map. Compare it with the size of the Arctic Ocean. Compare it with the size of Antarctica on page 38.

Pacific Ocean

Bering Sea

Sea of Okhotsk

UNITED STATES OF AMERICA (Alaska)

Bering Strait

RUSSIAN FEDERATION (RUSSIA)

CANADA

Beaufort Sea

New Siberian Islands

Arctic

North Pole

Severnaya Zemlya

Ocean

Baffin Bay

Franz Josef Land

Novaya Zemlya

Spitsbergen

GREENLAND

Barents Sea

Nuuk ■

Mount Forel ▲

Arctic Circle

ICELAND

NORWAY

Atlantic Ocean

British Isles

Zenithal Equidistant Projection
© Oxford University Press

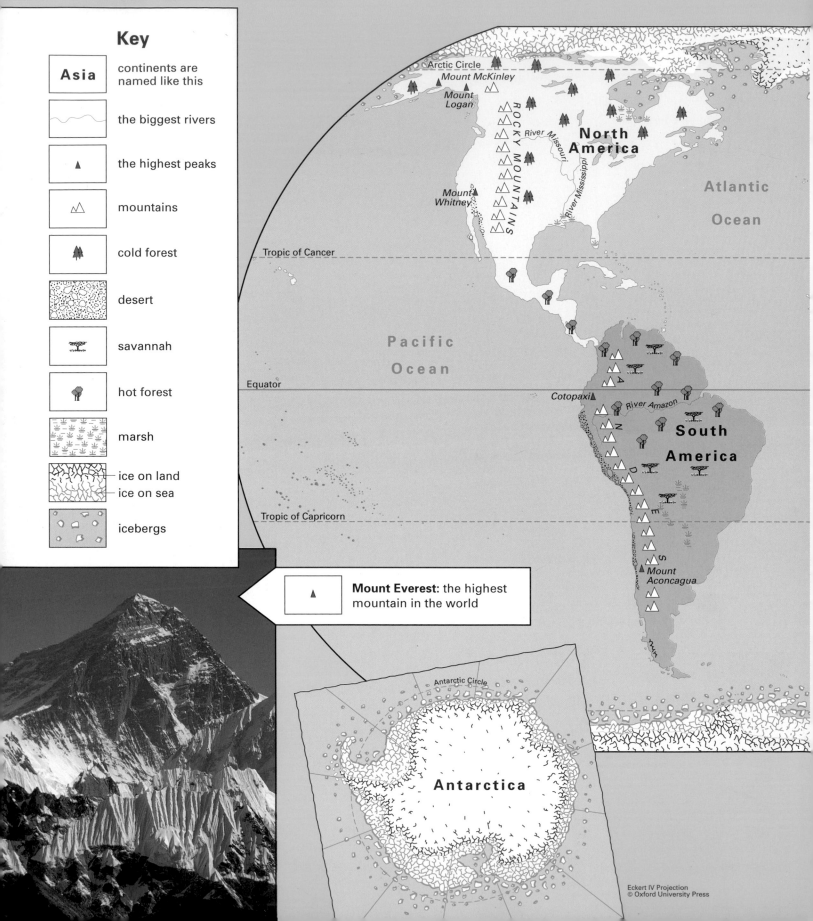

Key

Asia	continents are named like this
	the biggest rivers
▲	the highest peaks
/\\	mountains
🌲	cold forest
	desert
	savannah
🌳	hot forest
	marsh
	ice on land ice on sea
	icebergs

▲ **Mount Everest:** the highest mountain in the world

Arctic Circle

Mount McKinley

Mount Logan

ROCKY MOUNTAINS

River Missouri

North America

River Mississippi

Mount Whitney

Tropic of Cancer

Atlantic Ocean

Pacific Ocean

Equator

Cotopaxi ▲

River Amazon

South America

Tropic of Capricorn

A N D E S

Mount Aconcagua

Antarctic Circle

Antarctica

Eckert IV Projection
© Oxford University Press

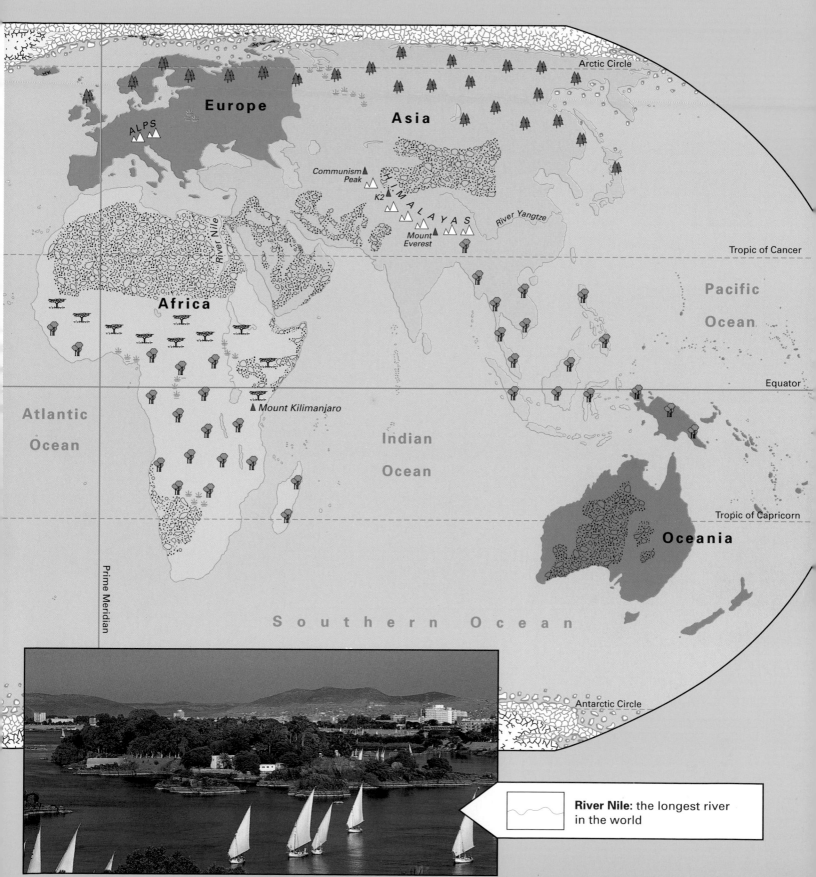

Arctic Circle

Europe

Asia

ALPS

Communism
Peak

K2 *HIMALAYAS*

River Yangtze

*Mount
Everest*

Tropic of Cancer

**Pacific
Ocean**

River Nile

Africa

**Atlantic
Ocean**

Equator

▲ Mount Kilimanjaro

**Indian
Ocean**

Tropic of Capricorn

Oceania

Prime Meridian

S o u t h e r n   O c e a n

Antarctic Circle

River Nile: the longest river
in the world

Eckert IV Projection
© Oxford University Press

Key

(gradient)	cold places
	cool places
	warm places
	hot places
☁	places with a lot of rain
☁❄	places with a lot of snow
(dots)	very dry places

Arctic Circle

Tropic of Cancer

Equator

Tropic of Capricorn

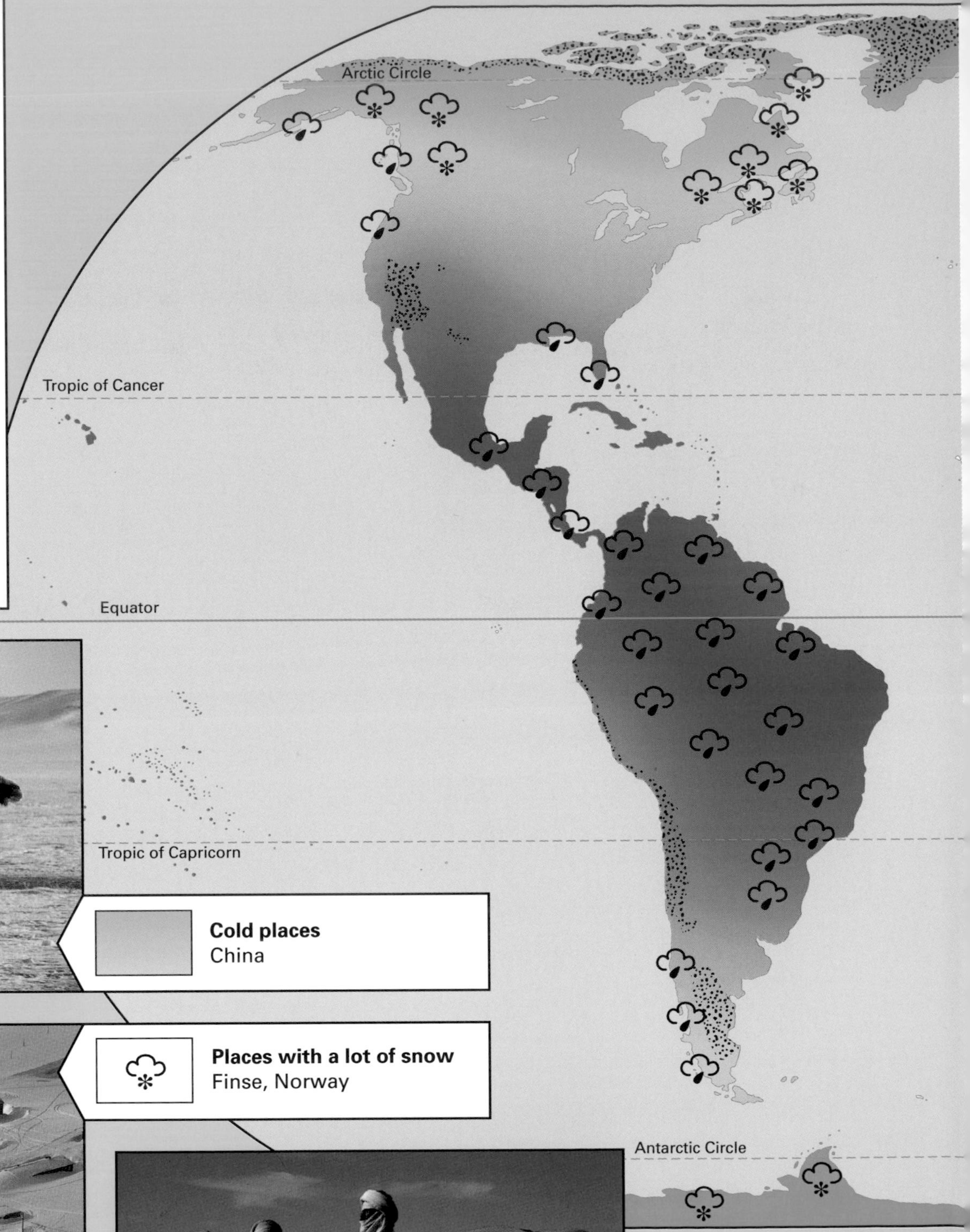

Cold places
China

Places with a lot of snow
Finse, Norway

Antarctic Circle

Very dry places
Sahara, Algeria

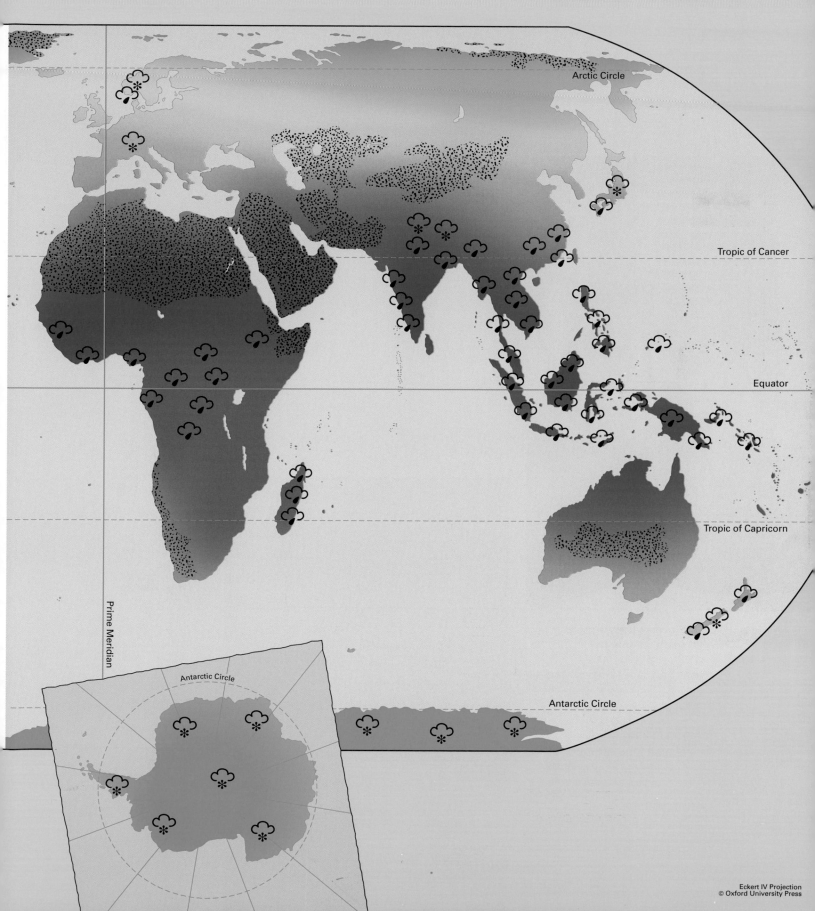

Arctic Circle

Tropic of Cancer

Equator

Prime Meridian

Tropic of Capricorn

Antarctic Circle

Antarctic Circle

Eckert IV Projection
© Oxford University Press

Key

One million (1 000 000)
people live near each dot

○ the world's largest cities

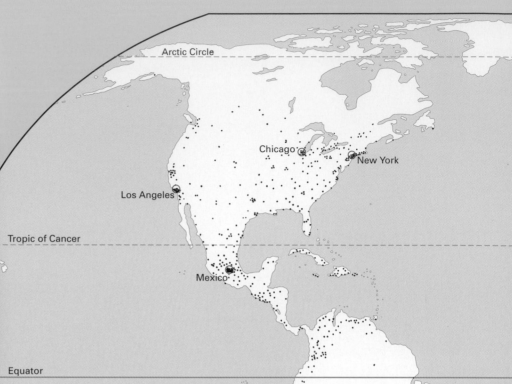

Arctic Circle

Chicago ◎

New York ◎

Los Angeles ◎

Tropic of Cancer

Mexico ◎

Equator

Tropic of Capricorn

São Paulo ◎

Buenos ◎
Aires

Antarctic Circle

**Places where very
many people live.**
Singapore

**Places where very
few people live.**
Shetland Islands,
United Kingdom

Eckert IV Projection
© Oxford University Press

Arctic Circle

Moscow

London

Paris

Beijing

Seoul

Tokyo

Delhi

Shanghai

Tropic of Cancer

Mumbai
(Bombay)

Calcutta

Equator

Tropic of Capricorn

Prime Meridian

Antarctic Circle

Antarctic Circle

Eckert IV Projection
© Oxford University Press

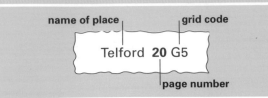

name of place · grid code

Telford **20** G5

page number